CONTENTS

THE WORKSHOP

BEFORE YOU START any of the projects, it is important that you learn a few simple rules about the care of your science factory.

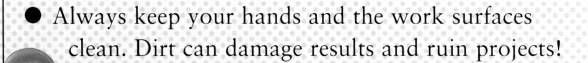

- Always keep your hands and the work surfaces clean. Dirt can damage results and ruin projects!

- Read the instructions carefully before you start each project.

- Make sure you have all the equipment you need for the project (see checklist opposite).

- If you haven't got the right piece of equipment, then improvise. For example, a washing-up liquid bottle will do just as well as a plastic drinks bottle.

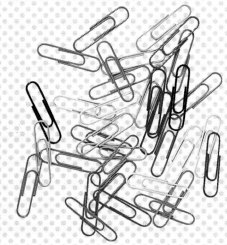

- Don't be afraid to make mistakes. Just start again – patience is very important!

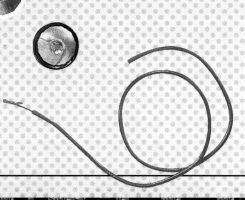

SCIENCE FACTORY

ELECTRICITY & BATTERIES

MICHAEL FLAHERTY

FRANKLIN WATTS
LONDON • SYDNEY

© Aladdin Books Ltd 1999

Designed and produced by
Aladdin Books Ltd
28 Percy Street
London W1P 0LD

ISBN 0 7496 3415 4 (hardcover)
ISBN 0 7496 4722 1 (paperback)

First published in Great Britain
in 1999 by
Aladdin/Watts Books
96 Leonard Street
London EC2A 4RH

Design

David West
Children's Book Design

Designer
Flick Killerby

Illustrators
Ian Moores and Ian Thompson

Printed in the U.A.E.

Some of the illustrations in this series
have appeared in previous titles
published by Aladdin Books.

The author, Michael Flaherty, has
written a number of science and
technology books for children.

The consultant, Steve Parker, has
worked on over 150 books for
children, mainly on a science theme.

All the photos in this book were
taken by Roger Vlitos.

INTRODUCTION

Electricity and Batteries looks at the basic aspects of electricity, as well as its more complex and practical uses. By following the projects, readers can develop their practical skills, while expanding their scientific knowledge. Other ideas then offer them the chance to explore each aspect further to build up a more comprehensive understanding of the subject.

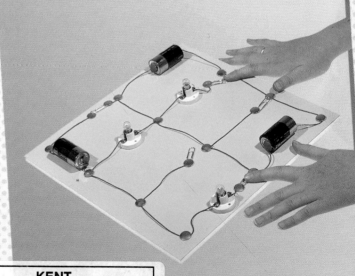

Equipment checklist:
- Scissors and glue
- Table-tennis balls
- Woollen cloth
- String and sticks
- Sweet wrapper foil and aluminium foil
- 6 volt bulbs and bulb holders
- Paper, cardboard and tissue paper
- Modelling clay and sticky-backed plastic
- Insulated wire
- Plastic drinking straws
- Paperclips and safety pins
- 1.5 volt batteries
- Drawing pins and nails
- Polystyrene blocks and boards
- Metal coat hanger
- Plastic lids, split pins and pencil lead
- Glass jar with cork lid
- Copper coins

WARNING:
Some of the experiments in this book need the help of an adult. Always ask a grown-up to give you a hand when you are using sharp objects, such as drawing pins, or electrical appliances!

STATIC ELECTRICITY

THERE ARE TWO MAIN FORMS OF ELECTRICITY – static (still) and current (flowing). Some materials do not let electricity pass through them, but a static electrical charge is produced on their surface when they rub against certain other materials. When you take off your jumper, you may hear a crackling sound as you produce static electricity. Make frogs jump by static electricity.

WHAT YOU NEED
Tissue paper
Coloured card
Table-tennis ball
String
Stick
Woollen cloth
Scissors

FROLICKING FROGS

1 *Fold a piece of tissue paper a number of times and cut out the shape of a frog. This way you can cut out more than one frog at the same time.*

2 *Cut out two lily-pad shapes from green card. Cut out some flowers, too. Put the lily pads on a piece of blue card for the pond. Place the frogs on one lily pad.*

3 *Cut a bird shape out of yellow card. Thread string through the bird and a table-tennis ball to join them together.*

4 *Tie the other end of the string to the end of the stick. Make sure that the bird rests on top of the ball.*

5 *Rub the table-tennis ball against something woollen. This gives the ball an electrical charge.*

WHY IT WORKS

The atoms which make up materials have negatively charged electrons and positively charged protons. When you rub the ball, you rub off electrons, leaving the ball with a positive charge. Because unlike charges attract each other, the positively charged ball attracts the paper frogs which have a negative charge in relation to the ball.

STICKY BALLOONS

Rub a balloon against something woollen. Hold it against a painted door and let go. The balloon seems stuck to the door. It is held to the wall by static electricity. The charge slowly disappears. How long does the effect last?

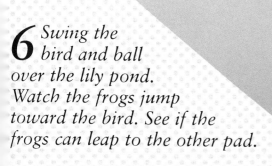

6 Swing the bird and ball over the lily pond. Watch the frogs jump toward the bird. See if the frogs can leap to the other pad.

DETECTING A CHARGE

In the last project, we saw how static electricity can be made through rubbing. In 1895, an apparatus called a gold leaf electroscope was invented to detect static electrical charge. You can build an apparatus like a primitive electroscope that shows you if a material is charged with static electricity or not.

WHAT YOU NEED

Bare wire
Aluminium foil
Jar with cork lid
Thin foil sweet-wrapper
Balloon

PRIMITIVE ELECTROSCOPE

1 Push a piece of wire through a large cork. Bend one end of the wire to make an L shape.

2 Roll a piece of aluminium foil into a ball and push it onto the top of the wire that's sticking out of the cork.

WHY IT WORKS

By rubbing the balloon you rub off some of its electrons and make it charged with static.

When it comes near to the aluminium foil ball, electrons in the wrapper are attracted to the balloon and move toward it and into the aluminium ball. This leaves the metal foil in the jar positively charged. The two wings of foil try to repel each other and push apart, so the foil moves.

3 Fold a piece of thin foil from a sweet wrapper in half and rest it on the bottom of the L-shaped wire. Put the cork in the jar, sealing the wrapper inside the jar.

4 Blow up a balloon and rub it on your jumper. Bring it near to the aluminium ball. Can you see the wrapper moving?

PUSHY BALLOONS

Blow up two balloons and rub them on a woollen cloth to charge them. Then hang them up by thread close to each other. Because you have rubbed electrons from the balloons onto the wool, the balloons are both positively charged. As a result, they repel one another and push apart.

9

A SIMPLE CIRCUIT

TODAY, WE CAN GENERATE large amounts of electricity. Metal wires and cables carry electricity from power stations to our homes. The electricity travels along these wires like water in a pipe. By switching on a light, you are completing one of these pathways, called a circuit. Electricity now flows through the electrical appliance you have switched on. The project below lets you set up your own circuit.

WHAT YOU NEED

6V bulb in holder
Insulated wire
Thin bare wire
Drinking straw
1.5V batteries
Polystyrene
Wire coat hanger

1 Screw a small 6V bulb into a bulb holder and attach a length of insulated wire to each side of the holder.

2 Make a piece of thin bare wire into a loop. Connect the loop and a long piece of insulated wire together. Thread a plastic straw onto the wire, and cover the join with the straw to form a handle.

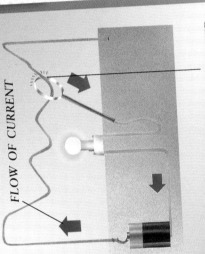

FLOW OF CURRENT

CIRCUIT IS COMPLETED

WHY IT WORKS

The electrons won't flow around the circuit until it is complete. By touching the loop to the hanger wire, you complete the circuit, and the bulb lights up as the electrons flow. Electrons flow from the negative end of the battery around the wire to the positive end of the battery.

3 Ask an adult to open up a wire coat hanger and bend it into bumps and curves. Attach one wire from the bulb to one end of the coat hanger. Attach the other wire from the bulb to two batteries which have been taped together.

4 Attach the wire loop to the other end of the batteries. You can use modelling clay or sticky tape to hold the wires on the ends of the batteries.

5 Thread the wire loop onto the free end of the hanger. Then stick the hanger into the polystyrene block. Try to move the loop along the coat hanger without them touching.

If you touch the coat hanger, the bulb will light up. See how far you can get!

SHORT CIRCUIT

Set up a simple circuit by connecting bare wires from the bulb to the battery. Then lay a metal object, such as a spoon, across the wires. The bulb goes out. You have made a short circuit.

SWITCHING ON

A SWITCHED CIRCUIT is a circuit where the flow of electricity is controlled by a switch. When the switch is open, or off, there is a gap in the circuit and the electricity doesn't flow. Electricity flows when the switch is closed, or on. In this project, you can use switches to send messages to your friends using flashing lights to make the letters in code.

WHAT YOU NEED

Polystyrene
Modelling clay
Two 6V bulbs
and holders
1.5V batteries
Insulated wire
Drawing pins
Paperclips

SECRET MESSAGES

1 *Put a bulb in each bulb holder and attach the holders to separate polystyrene boards. Connect the bulb holders to each other using a long wire.*

2 *On each board, connect the sockets to a drawing pin holding a paperclip. Add another drawing pin within reach of each paperclip. These will be your switches.*

3 *On each board, connect the second drawing pin to one end of a battery. Now connect the other ends of the batteries to each other using a long piece of wire. Make sure that the two ends of the batteries which you are connecting are different, otherwise electricity will not flow.*

MORSE CODE

You can send messages to a friend using Morse Code, by making the bulbs flash on and off quickly for dots and more slowly for dashes.

a	•–	s	•••
b	–•••	t	–
c	–•–•	u	••–
d	–••	v	•••–
e	•	w	•––
f	••–•	x	–••–
g	––•	y	–•––
h	••••	z	––••
i	••	1	•––––
j	•–––	2	••–––
k	–•–	3	•••––
l	•–••	4	••••–
m	––	5	•••••
n	–•	6	–••••
o	–––	7	––•••
p	•––•	8	–––••
q	––•–	9	––––•
r	•–•	0	–––––

4 When the paperclip switches are touching the drawing pins, the bulbs will light up. Keep one switch closed, and open and close the other to send a signal down the wire.

When the paperclips are in contact with the drawing pins the circuit is complete and electrons can flow, lighting the bulbs. To send a signal down the wire, the sender must raise and lower one of the paperclips to open and close the circuit. This is shown by the light bulbs going on and off.

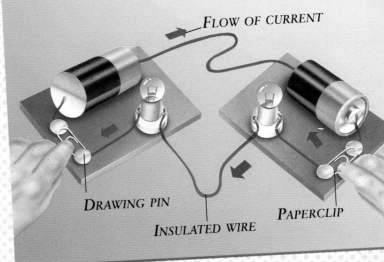

FLOW OF CURRENT

DRAWING PIN

INSULATED WIRE

PAPERCLIP

Two-Way Switches

Two-way switches allow you to turn an appliance, such as a light in your house, off and on from two different places. You may have a stairway light which you can turn on and off at the top and at the bottom of the stairs. Build your own two-way switch in this experiment and see how it works.

What you need
Drawing pins
Thick board
Two plastic lids
Paperclips
Two 1.5V batteries
6V bulb in holder
Insulated wire
Modelling clay

ON AND OFF

1 *Make a hole in the top of a lid. Push the wires that you have connected to a bulb through the hole.*

2 *Open a paperclip and tape one end inside the lid so that the other end sticks out. Attach one wire to the paperclip and the other to the batteries (below).*

5 *Position the lids and twist them so the paperclip switches can touch the drawing pins connected to the wires (above). The bulb will go on and off as the switches are opened and closed between both wires.*

14

3 Place four drawing pins in a board, two at each end, and connect them in pairs with two pieces of wire, as shown. Place other drawing pins near them to hold the two plastic lids in place.

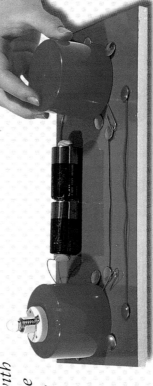

4 Form a switch with a paperclip in the other lid in the same way. Connect it to the other end of the batteries.

LOWERING SWITCHES

There are other uses for two-way switches. A person in a wheelchair may need a light switch lower down the wall at a height that he or she can reach. Design a two-way switch circuit which would suit this purpose.

WHY IT WORKS

A two-way switch allows you to turn a light off and on in two different places. This is because there are two possible pathways for the electricity to flow along. These are the two wires (blue and red) you built into your circuit. For electricity to flow, both switches must be turned to the same pathway, either the blue or the red wire.

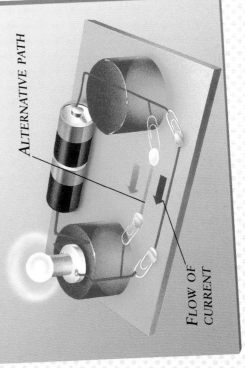

ALTERNATIVE PATH

FLOW OF CURRENT

LIGHTING THE DARK

IN 1879, AMERICAN INVENTOR Thomas Edison made the first electric light bulb. For the filament, the part that glows when electricity is passed through it, he used a piece of cotton thread heated to a black strip. He removed the air from the bulb and turned on the current. The bulb glowed. By 1913, a metal called tungsten was used as the filament.

ELECTRONIC QUIZ

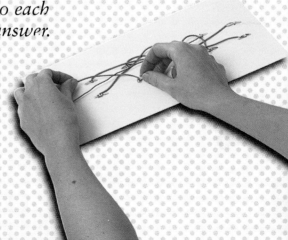

1 *Make up some questions and answers, and write each on a separate piece of paper.*

2 *Glue the questions in one column on one side of a piece of card. Glue the answers in a random order in another column on the card.*

5 *Make a circuit with more wire, a battery and a bulb. Leave the ends of the wires free.*

3 *Push a split pin through the card next to each question and each answer.*

4 *On the back of the card, join the split pins of each question with a short length of wire to its correct answer.*

TRAFFIC LIGHTS

Build a circuit with three coloured lights to make traffic lights. Connect them together with switches so that they can be turned on in different sequences depending on whether the traffic must stop or go.

6 Ask a friend a question and let him or her choose one of the answers. With the free ends of the wires in your circuit, touch the split pins next to the question and the answer your friend gives. If the bulb lights up, the answer is correct.

WHY IT WORKS

Each question's split pin is connected by wire to the split pin of the correct answer. By touching the wires of your circuit to a question and its answer, you complete the circuit so electricity flows and the bulb lights up. If the answer is wrong, the circuit is not completed, and the bulb will not light up.

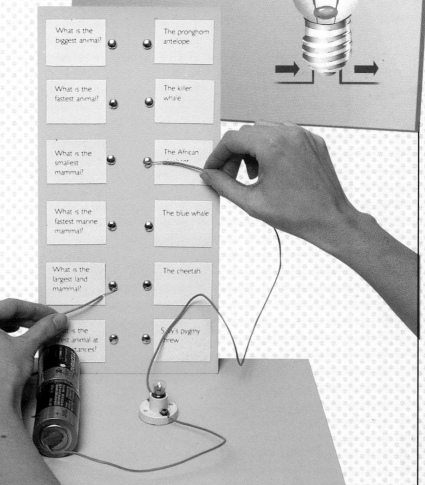

CONDUCTORS

WHAT YOU NEED
Thick board
Aluminium foil
Insulated wire
Sticky-backed plastic
Two 1.5V batteries
Bulb in holder
Nail

SOME MATERIALS WILL NOT ALLOW ELECTRICITY to flow along them. They are called insulators. Other materials will let a current pass through them. These are called conductors. We need conductors to make electric wires and circuits, while insulators are important in protecting us from dangerous electric currents. This project will show you the difference between conductors and insulators.

3 *Before you stick down a final conducting path, make a hole near the edge of the board and insert the end of some insulated wire.*

ELECTRIC MAZE

1 *Cut a piece of aluminium foil the same size as your board. Cover the foil with a sheet of clear sticky-backed plastic.*

2 *Design your maze on the board, and cut out strips of plastic-covered foil to fit your paths. Stick them down plastic side up. These are your insulated paths.*

4 *Attach the other end of the wire to a battery. To the other terminal of the battery, attach a wire leading to a bulb in a holder. Attach another piece of wire to the other side of the holder and put a nail on the end of it.*

TESTING

You can test other materials to see if they are conductors using your circuit. Touch the free ends of the wires to the ends of objects made from different materials, such as rubbers and spoons.

When the nail touches the plastic, the bulb goes out. The plastic is an insulator and blocks the current. The electrons in an insulator are not free to move as they are in a conductor, such as aluminium foil, so the current doesn't flow.

NAIL

FOIL PATHWAY

FLOW OF CURRENT

5 Cut out your final conducting path and stick it to your board, foil side up. Make sure the wire contacts the foil at one end. Let your friends find their way through the maze.

POOR CONDUCTORS AND RESISTORS

NOT ALL CONDUCTORS ARE EQUAL. An electrical current can pass through some more easily than others. The thinner the wire, the higher the resistance, like the slower flow of water through pipes of different widths. Resistance also varies with length. In the experiment below you can test different conductors to see if they have high or low resistance.

WHAT YOU NEED
Bulb in holder
Insulated wire
Thick board
Cardboard
Paperclip
Pencil lead
1.5V batteries
Drawing pins
Aluminium foil

WOOD

Replace the lead in the experiment with a wooden skewer that has been soaked in salt water overnight. The salt in the water should allow the wood to conduct electricity. As the wood begins to dry out, the resistance will increase until eventually the wood will stop conducting.

RESISTANCE

1 Set up a circuit like the one shown, using insulated wire, drawing pins and a bulb in a holder. Get some lead from a self-propelling pencil, and cut out two pieces of thick card to rest it on.

2 *To reflect the light, make a shade from a cardboard disc and aluminium foil.*

3 *Cut a slit in the disc and glue it into a cone shape. Cut a hole in the centre of the cone and place it over the bulb.*

20

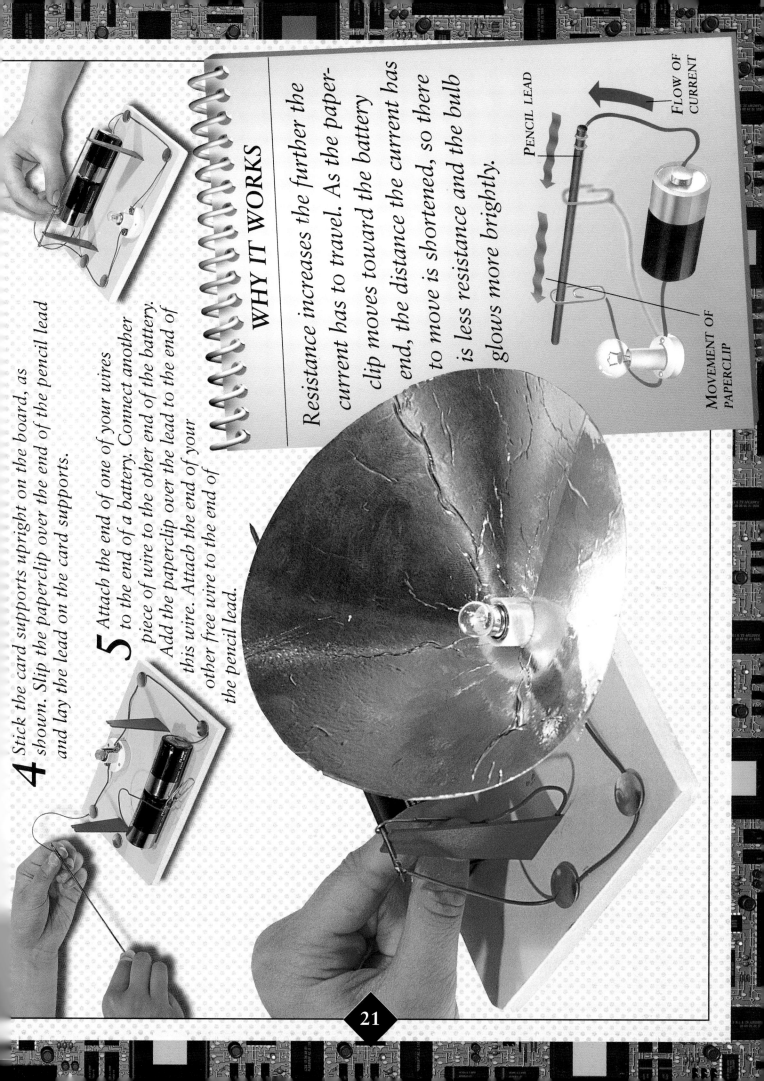

4 Stick the card supports upright on the board, as shown. Slip the paperclip over the end of the pencil lead and lay the lead on the card supports.

5 Attach the end of one of your wires to the end of a battery. Connect another piece of wire to the other end of the battery. Add the paperclip over the lead to the end of this wire. Attach the end of your other free wire to the end of the pencil lead.

WHY IT WORKS

Resistance increases the further the current has to travel. As the paper-clip moves toward the battery end, the distance the current has to move is shortened, so there is less resistance and the bulb glows more brightly.

FLOW OF CURRENT

PENCIL LEAD

MOVEMENT OF PAPERCLIP

VOLTAGE AND CIRCUITS

IF YOU PUT MANY BULBS in a circuit in a line, so that one leads on after the other, they are said to be in series. If one of the bulbs goes out, they all go out. Streetlights in the early 1900s were set up like this, and streets were plunged into darkness when one of the lights failed. The solution was to put them in parallel, so that the current didn't have to go through one bulb to get to another. Streetlights today are in parallel circuits, so that if one lamp fails, the others will continue to glow.

WHY IT WORKS

A series circuit uses one path to connect the bulb and the battery. If two batteries are used, the bulb glows twice as brightly. Two bulbs in a series circuit glow less brightly than just one. A parallel circuit has more than one path for the current. Each bulb receives the current at the same force, or voltage, no matter how many bulbs there are in parallel. If a bulb burns out, the others continue to glow because their circuits are not broken.

DIRECTION OF FLOW

SERIES AND PARALLEL

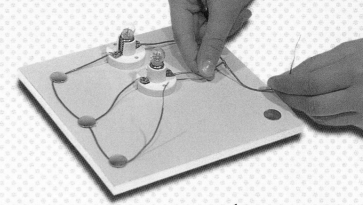

1 Set up a circuit with two bulbs in parallel, connecting the bare ends of the wires to drawing pins as shown. Attach the free ends of the wire to the ends of a battery. Both bulbs glow with equal brightness.

2 Now remove one of the bulbs. The other should stay alight.

3 Now set up a circuit with two batteries connected end to end, in series. Connect them to a single bulb. How brightly does it glow? Take one of the batteries out. How brightly is the bulb glowing now?

OTHER CIRCUITS

Using the parallel circuit that you made in the project, replace the bulb in the middle of the circuit with a battery, as shown here. How does this affect the bulb? Does it glow brighter or dimmer? Or does it not glow at all?

23

THE HOME CIRCUIT

HOMES TODAY CONTAIN PARALLEL CIRCUITS. One of these circuits has sockets in the walls. Lights can be run off a separate circuit. All lights and appliances are connected in parallel so that everything operates at the same voltage; turning things on and off does not change the voltage to other appliances. Experiment with more complex circuits in the project below.

WHAT YOU NEED
Large board
Three bulbs
Three 1.5V batteries
Insulated wire
Drawing pins
Modelling clay
Paperclips

SWITCHES AND LIGHTS

1 Place batteries at three corners of the board. Make sure that unlike terminals are facing each other. Attach wires using modelling clay.

2 Connect the bulbs to the batteries using short lengths of wire running between drawing pins as shown. Leave gaps in the circuits for switches made from paperclips and drawing pins.

WHY IT WORKS

The flow of electrons is controlled by closing and opening the switches. A bulb stops glowing when the electrons no longer flow through it. All the bulbs will glow when every switch is connected (closed).

BULB IN COMPLETED CIRCUIT

ISOLATED BULB

SWITCHING BATTERIES

Experiment with the way the batteries are facing. Turn one around and see how it affects the rest of the circuit. Can all the bulbs be lit up now? Do the bulbs glow as brightly as before? Remember that electrons flow from negative to positive only.

3 *Close the paperclip switches and see the bulbs light up. How brightly are the bulbs glowing?*

4 *By opening and closing certain switches, can you have just one light bulb on? Experiment with the switches to see if you can get only two to light up. Do the bulbs glow at different degrees of brightness?*

MAGNETISM

IN THE 1820S A DANISH SCIENTIST NAMED HANS CHRISTIAN OERSTED found a link between electricity and magnetism. He noticed that a magnetic compass needle was deflected when an electric wire was held near it. He soon realised that an electric current flowing through a wire creates a magnetic field. You too can make an electromagnet in the project below.

ELECTROMAGNETIC FACE

1 Push a nail through the centre of a piece of board. Wrap wire around the nail at least 20 times, leaving the two ends the same length.

WHY IT WORKS

The current flows through the wire coiled around the nail and turns it into a magnet. The clown's nose is held in place because the drawing pin is attracted to the magnetic field. When the electricity is turned off, the magnetic field disappears and the nose falls off.

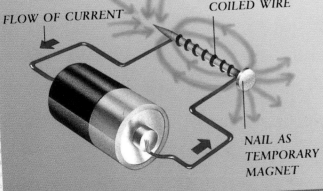

FLOW OF CURRENT

COILED WIRE

NAIL AS TEMPORARY MAGNET

2 Cut two triangular pieces of polystyrene to support the board in a sloping position.

3 Attach the triangles as shown. Pierce a small hole in the side of one of the triangles to fit a paperclip through.

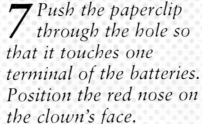

7 Push the paperclip through the hole so that it touches one terminal of the batteries. Position the red nose on the clown's face.

8 While the paperclip is touching the batteries the circuit is complete and the nose will stick to the clown's face.

4 Draw a clown's face on a second piece of polystyrene board. Do not draw a nose on the face. Colour the face and cut it out to fit over your sloping board.

5 Colour a table-tennis ball red to make a clown's nose and push a drawing pin into it.

6 Position two batteries inside the shape as shown. Connect one of the wires from the nail to one end of the batteries. Connect the other wire to the paper clip. Glue the face board to the top of the shape.

MAGNETIC LINES

Pierce the centre of a piece of card with a piece of wire. Sprinkle some iron filings onto the card. Attach both ends of the wire to two connected batteries. The iron filings will line up in concentric circles, showing the 'lines of force' of the magnetic field.

ELECTRICITY AND IONS

AN ELECTRICAL CURRENT can pass through liquids, such as a salt solution, causing a chemical reaction. This is called electrolysis. Two metal plates, called electrodes, deliver the current to the liquid (electrolyte). Electrolysis is used to coat metallic objects with a thin layer of a more expensive, attractive or hard-wearing metal. This process is called electroplating.

WHAT YOU NEED
Glass jar of salt water
Copper coin
Paperclip
Two 1.5V batteries
Insulated wire
Modelling clay

ELECTROPLATING

1 Connect the two batteries with the unlike terminals touching. Connect insulated wire to the free terminals. Attach the copper coin to the wire from the positive battery terminal.

2 Attach a paperclip to the wire from the negative battery terminal. Fill the jar with salt water and place the coin and the paperclip in the water. They will act as the electrodes.

SALT AND VINEGAR

Try the experiment again using a solution of salt dissolved in vinegar. Do you notice any difference? Does anything happen to the paperclip? Add more batteries in parallel to increase the 'pressure' of the current.

WHY IT WORKS

The electricity flows through the solution as charged particles called ions. Copper ions carry the positive charge towards the negative paperclip where they pick up electrons and are deposited on the paperclip as a thin layer of copper.

CURRENT FLOWS THROUGH THE SOLUTION, CARRYING COPPER IONS TO THE PAPERCLIP

3 *Watch closely to see what happens. Are there bubbles forming? Leave the coin and the paperclip for a few minutes before taking them out. Are there any colour changes? Put them back in the water for a while longer. Can you see any more changes?*

FINDING OUT MORE

CONDUCTOR A material that will allow electrons to flow through it. Examples include metals and carbon. *Experiment with different conductors on pages 18-19.*

ELECTRIC CIRCUIT The path around which an electrical current flows. It includes a source of electricity, such as a battery. *You can make a simple circuit in the project on pages 10-11.*

ELECTRIC CURRENT The movement of electrons along a wire. *Make a current flow in the project on pages 10-11.*

ELECTRODE When sending an electric current through a liquid, such as a salt solution, the electricity is carried into the liquid by two conductors called electrodes. *See how electrodes are used on pages 28-29.*

ELECTRIC EEL

There are 500 types of fish that generate electricity. The electric eel of South America is the largest and produces the most electricity – to detect and stun prey.

LIGHTNING

A flash of lightning travels at almost the speed of light. It can be as much as 100 million volts and heat the air in its path to 33,000°C!

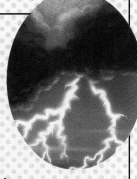

DAMS

The Itaipu Dam in South America produces enough electricity to supply Paraguay with over three quarters of its needs and Brazil with one quarter of its needs.

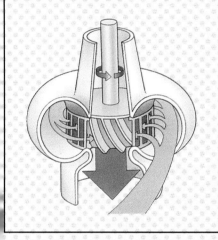

ELECTROMAGNET

An iron or steel object surrounded by a coil of wire that acts like a magnet when a current flows through the wire. *Make your own electromagnet in the project on pages 26-27.*

ELECTRON One of the tiny particles that make up atoms. Electrons have a negative charge. Whether moving or static, electrons are what we call electricity. *Find out more about electrons in the project on pages 8-9.*

ION A charged particle in a fluid. *Use ions to carry electrical charge through a salt solution in the project on pages 28-29.*

STATIC ELECTRICITY

A type of electricity that forms on the surface of certain materials that are rubbed together. *Experiment with static electricity in the projects on pages 6-9.*

VOLTAGE The force that pushes electricity through a wire, similar to the pressure of water in a pipe. *Experiment with voltage on pages 22-23.*

SOLAR POWER

In Odeilo, France, huge mirrors are used to concentrate the Sun's light to heat water into steam. This steam drives a turbine to produce electricity.

INDEX